I0161259

RED

MEANS

GO!

**Secrets To Achieving A Happy,
Effective And Successful Life
With You In The Drivers Seat**

CARL TAYLOR

Red Means Go! Secrets to achieving a happy, effective and successful life with you in the driver's seat © Carl Taylor 2010
www.carltaylor.com.au

First Published in Australia 2010 by Kaizen Publishing
www.kaizenbookpublishing.com

National Library of Australia
Cataloguing-in-Publication entry:

Taylor, Carl.

   Red means go! : secrets to achieving a happy, effective and successful life with you in the driver's seat / by Carl Taylor ; illustrations by Roger Harvey.

   9780980763201 (pbk.)

   Self-actualization (Psychology)
   Happiness.
   Success.

   Harvey, Roger, 1956-

158.1

ISBN 978-0-9807632-0-1

Illustrations by Roger Harvey [rogerharvey.net]
Cover design by Daniel Yeager [nu-images.com]
Printed and bound by Griffin Press [griffinpress.com.au]

To my friends and family, may you learn to love life and its amazing possibilities

---

To those who are ready to take control of their life, may you learn to transform your life and share what you learn with anybody and everybody that you meet

Acknowledgements

Writing this book has been a long time coming. It's been a joy to write, as I've learned so much and have been bursting at the seams to educate others. Now it is time to acknowledge those who have contributed to my being and learning.

To all the writers of all the books, the teachers of all the seminars and the mistake makers who lead the way, thank you.

To my sister, Alison, thank you for being a challenger of my positivity. You keep me grounded and always learning.

To all my friends, thanks for the interesting conversations, the motivating inspiration and most importantly the fun we always have.

And finally, to Mum and Dad, thank you for your support and instilling the culture in me that I can do anything I put my mind to.

Contents

Y ou've felt it, haven't you? That feeling that life could be so much more?

You see people around you that just seem LUCKY. They love life, achieve great things and everybody loves them. Do you wonder to yourself, "What's their secret?"

I used to feel that way. Everything was out of my control. I had to just coast through life with whatever hand I was dealt.

I'm here to tell you something: you don't need to feel that way. You don't need to accept that. That is a complete load of $#!%.

In this book, you will learn what those people either consciously or unconsciously know.

And I promise you, when you take what you are about to learn and put it into consistent daily practice, your life is going to change dramatically.

Chapter One

START YOUR ENGINE
The Philosophy of Kaizen

> *Never wish your life were easier;*
> *wish that you were better*
>
> – Jim Rohn

There are $183 of Bonus Gifts Waiting for You...

There is a philosophy that people all around the world are living by. It's known as *Kaizen*.

What is Kaizen?

The term Kaizen is Japanese for "improvement" or "continuous improvement." The English language has adopted it when referring to a philosophy or practice that focuses on continuous improvement in all areas of life.

The concept of continuous improvement has been around for thousands of years in the Japanese culture.

After World War II, the Kaizen philosophy was originally brought into the Western world by the car manufacturer Toyota, who implemented this philosophy as a part of their manufacturing process.

But how does the philosophy of Kaizen apply to you?

Easy. Take the words "continuous improvement." Now add the word "self" right in the middle.

What do you have now? "Continuous self-improvement."

Applying Kaizen

We all have things we want to change in our life, whether we want more or specific material objects or want something more on a philosophical level. Maybe you're looking for more social interactions or changes. Whatever it is you want, I'm here to tell you that with Kaizen, you can get it.

I suggest to you that the best way to reach this better world that you desire is to become a more effective person, and you can only become a more effective person through Kaizen.

Self-improvement is common and is easily achieved. However, "continuous self-improvement" is actually unachievable because you will never get to a point where you say, "I've achieved continuous self-improvement," because at that point, it would no longer be continuous. Does that concept confuse you? Do you wonder why you should bother trying to do something if it's unachievable?

Let me explain...

Continuous self-improvement is unachievable, but the striving for, the journey towards it, that is the single most effective way to approach your personal paradise. It's where you will decide the cards in your hand, not let someone else deal you any old card that is available.

Let me stress this to you!!!

By striving for continuous self-improvement, you will change your world. As the great Jim Rohn said, "Never wish your life were easier; wish that you were better."

There are $183 of Bonus Gifts Waiting for You...

He was 100% right, because guess what? The better you become, the easier life actually becomes.

Kaizen and Wealth

Some of the wealthiest people in the world love personal development. They work harder on themselves than they do on their jobs, businesses or investments.

But if you ask them, "What is wealth?" you may be surprised by the answer. It's not riches in monetary form, but life wealth—living a rich, fulfilled and happy life.

You see, true financial independence is not having a billion dollars sitting safely in a bank account, but actually having the power to produce wealth. And that power comes from continuous self-improvement.

A Key to Sticking to this Path of Kaizen...

Be interested in Kaizen. Have a passion for self-improvement. Want to do it.

Let's think of it in another way.

Your child comes home from school. It was report card day today, and he sheepishly hands you his report card. His teachers all say the same thing: "Charlie is a capable student, but is too easily distracted from his tasks and could apply more effort."

He's not passing his subjects. You try to talk with him about it, and his answer is simple.

"I can just never remember what we learn in class."

Now let's ask Charlie about his favourite soccer player. Charlie quickly rattles off scores and statistics that he can remember and his face lights up. Isn't it interesting? He can't remember what he learns in class, but he has no trouble remembering what some might see as useless facts.

What's the difference?

Interest!!!!

Charlie has no interest in what school is teaching, but when it comes to soccer, those facts aren't meaningless to him. They are something he is passionate about. He loves them, and they consume him.

So the key to successfully taking on the philosophy of Kaizen is to become passionate and interested in the journey of continuous self-improvement. That way, you will be just like Charlie with his soccer stats: eager, excited and wanting to learn more.

Why should you become so interested in Kaizen and the journey of continuous self-improvement?

Maybe you just want to change a few areas in your life. Why should you become so passionate about improving yourself all around?

Because it's all interrelated.

There are $183 of Bonus Gifts Waiting for You...

Physical health affects your mental health; emotional strength affects your relationships; and it goes on and on...

By improving in one area of your life, you increase your ability in other areas as well.

Now isn't that exciting?

By making one change, you are actually affecting numerous areas of your life!

There is another great saying I just love, and you will find that I like quite a few sayings. They are spread all throughout this book.

"The more you LEARN, the more your EARN."

So congratulations. By reading this book, you have made a commitment.

Due to your commitment to reading the rest of this book, you will be LEARNING, and this learning will be compounding and increasing your EARNING in the richness and fullness of life that you will achieve and 110% deserve.

There are $183 of Bonus Gifts Waiting for You...

Chapter Two

LOOK UNDER THE HOOD

Understanding the way you think

“ *Imagination is more important than knowledge*

– Albert Einstein ”

There are $183 of Bonus Gifts Waiting for You...

Why do we do what we do?

How did we as human beings develop into the thinking machines that we are?

The Human Mind is an amazing biological machine. It has electricity running through it and it controls essentially every part of our body.

So if it is a machine, does it have certain rules and systems that it follows? I, along with many scientists and researchers, certainly believe so, and in this chapter, we are going to look at some of the key things you should know about how your mind works.

How we Learn

One of the most fascinating and mysterious properties of the brain is its capacity to learn. The ability to learn and to establish new memories is fundamental to our very existence. We rely on our memories to engage in actions, to understand the words here on this page, and to recognise objects and people that we see.

Did you know, however, that not everybody learns the same way that you do? In fact, one of the hardest truths we as humans struggle to grasp is that people don't think the same way that we do.

People learn in different ways. And no one has a better learning style than anyone else. We all just have different preferences.

To Claim Them visit www.KaizenSeries.com/RMG

There are three types of learning. These are known as VAK.

- Visual   (Seeing and Reading)

- Auditory   (Listening and Speaking)

- Kinaesthetic   (Touching and Doing)

According to the VAK model, most of us possess a dominant or preferred learning style. However, we all have a mixed, but not evenly balanced, blend of the three styles of learning.

For example, I know that, for myself, I am a Kinaesthetic and Visual Learner. I learn quickest and easiest when I just get into it and do it. I learn a little less quickly and easily if I'm shown it or see it done. But if someone just explains to me how to do something, I find it a lot harder to learn what is taught.

Why do you think it might be important to know what your dominant and preferred learning styles are?

That's right. Because when you know how you learn best, you can dramatically increase your rate of learning and help the people you engage to teach you to teach you more effectively.

One of the things that I look back on regarding my experience at school is that the education system doesn't seem to really take into account these different learning styles. I can remember classes where I sat there listening to a teacher go on about a subject, and because Auditory is not my dominant learning style at all, it really just went in one ear and out the other. However, if you made me write out a block of text from the textbook, I was able to absorb so much more. I was reading, so my Visual style was working away, and I was writing, so I was doing something physical, which appealed to my Kinaesthetic style as well.

You remember those kids in class. The teacher would shout at them to stop fidgeting. What most teachers don't realise is there is a reason they are fidgeting. Their minds need them to be doing some kind of action, not just sitting still so that they can absorb the information being taught.

So how do you find out what your learning styles are?

Try the following exercise... (Read through it first before starting.)

Close your eyes.

Imagine you are on a desert island. There are waves around you, the sun is in the sky, and it is a glorious day.

Now open your eyes.

(Do the exercise now before reading on.)

How did you feel? Describe on a piece of paper the experience you just created in your mind... What did you see, hear, and feel?

Now add up the number of times you described feelings, like "The sun felt warm on my back" or "I felt the sand in between my toes." Add up the times you described visuals, like "The sun was blinding and the sea was blue," and add up the number of times you described sounds, like "Birds were singing" or "Waves were crashing."

Which ones were the most dominant? Is it a surprise?

There are $183 of Bonus Gifts Waiting for You...

Did you struggle with that exercise?

Here are a few more questions you can try to help you if that exercise was a bit of a struggle.

When operating new equipment for the first time, I prefer to...

(A)   Read the instructions

(B)   Listen or ask for an explanation

(C)   Have a go and learn by trial and error

When seeking travel directions, I...

(A)   Look at a map

(B)   Ask for directions

(C)   Follow my nose or maybe use a compass or GPS

When cooking a new dish, I...

(A)   Follow a recipe

(B)   Call a friend for an explanation

(C)   Follow my instinct, tasting as I cook

Now what you will find here is A's are all Visual answers, B's are all Auditory and C's are all Kinaesthetic.

Remember, most of us are a bit of all three, but there are usually two that are dominant, and one is the most dominant.

So you now know your learning styles, but what about your friends, family and colleagues? Would it be useful to know which type of learning is best for them?

Absolutely. The more you know about people and how they learn and interact with the world, the deeper and better connections you can make with them. This is because you no longer impose your thoughts and view of the world on them. You actually understand that they see the world in a whole different way.

You can easily use the exercises above with close friends and family, but what about strangers that you meet? Is there a way you can detect what learning type they are?

There is a rough way that I use. It's not 100% accurate, but I've found it quite effective.

The next time you are saying goodbye to someone, listen carefully to what he/she says.

For example, let's look at a hypothetical situation between John and Sally.

John and Sally are saying their goodbyes. John says, "Sally, it was great seeing you. I'll talk to you soon." And Sally says, "Thanks, John. I'll catch you later."

Can you see what's occurred here? Can you see the subtleties in their language?

There are $183 of Bonus Gifts Waiting for You...

John has used two expressions that indicate a learning style. He has said, "It was great seeing you." This is a Visual indicator, and he has also said, "I'll talk to your soon," which is an Auditory indicator.

Sally, on the other hand, has said, "I'll catch you later." This is a physical action expression, so it is a Kinaesthetic indicator.

Isn't it interesting? You now have a better understanding of yourself and how you perceive the world around you. By knowing this about yourself, you can now make the right choices when you decide what parts of your life you want to focus on improving.

Think about this. If your lowest type of learning is Visual, then picking up a physical book and reading it is most likely going to be extremely boring and you won't really get anything out of it. In fact, if you are one of these people and you have managed to get to this point in this book, I'm impressed. But I recommend you put this book down right now and go and get either the audio book version or register for a seminar so that you get the most out of your learning investment.

Colours and Learning

Researchers from the University of Chicago and Vanderbilt University have uncovered that the brain plays a critical role in colour perception. According to their study, it is the brain – and not the eyes – that assigns colours to objects.

For many years, people have known that colours do affect us. They can affect how we feel and the way we think. Did you also know that colours can have an impact on our learning?

Let me explain how...

Colours send signals to the brain without us even thinking about it. Some are soothing, while some are not. Some help us focus, while some are distracting.

Fast food marketers have known this for a long time. Have you noticed the amount of fast food places that have red in their logos and colours? This is because red has been found to trigger a hunger response, which is what you would want if you were trying to run a business that feeds people.

Colour also influences the way we see and process information. It can improve our ability to remember both words and pictures. An experiment published in the Journal of Experimental Psychology showed some interesting results.

In the study, participants looked at 48 photographs, half in colour and half in black and white. Later, they viewed the same 48 images randomly mixed with 48 new images, and indicated whether they had seen each picture or not.

The results? Participants remembered colour photographs of natural scenes coloured normally significantly better than they remembered black and white images. However, those same participants didn't recall colour scenes coloured falsely any better than scenes in black and white. It wasn't just any colour that strengthened people's memory, but only the colours inherent to the scenes the photos depicted.

The result of that and other studies suggests that colour is vital to helping us in the retention of information. So, as we go through our journey of continuous self-improvement and learning, knowing the impact colour has on us is very important.

So when you are attending seminars or taking notes on something, don't just use your boring blue or black pen. Take a bunch of coloured text and choose your colours wisely. When you are making a note of what not to do, you may use red to indicate "stop," like a red traffic light. And when making notes about what to do, you may use green.

There are no hard and fast rules on what colours to use, but they should have a significance related with what you are applying them to. Another great impact of using colours while making notes is that if you ever get stuck with a thought, just change colours. A new colour triggers a mental shift, and your thoughts will start flowing again.

The Reticular Activating System (RAS)

The reticular activating system (RAS) is an area of the brain responsible for regulating attention.

Imagine that you are walking through a busy airport terminal. Think of all the noise – hundreds of people talking, music, announcements. How much of this noise is brought to your attention? Not a lot.

Yes, you do hear general background noise, but not many of us actually bother to listen to each individual sound.

But then an announcement comes over the PA, and it's calling your name or your flight. Suddenly, you are at full attention. Your RAS is the automatic mechanism inside your brain that brings relevant information to your attention.

Your RAS is like a filter between your conscious mind and your subconscious mind. It takes instructions from your conscious mind and then passes them to your subconscious.

Here's another example...

Do you remember when you bought your car? You felt so special. You had this great new car, and no one else had the same car. You're driving around and, all of a sudden, you notice that your model car is everywhere. Your neighbour

There are $183 of Bonus Gifts Waiting for You...

has it; there are heaps parked at the shop. Did everyone go out and buy your car at the same time you did? No, of course not; but you just never paid much attention to it. Now, however, your RAS is switched on to look for your car. It's something it recognises as being important to notice.

Maybe you haven't bought the car yet. Often, when you are looking to buy a new car, you start seeing the one you like everywhere.

So why is the RAS so important to us in our Kaizen journey?

Well, firstly, you can deliberately program the reticular activating system by choosing the exact messages you send from your conscious mind. For example, you can set a goal, say affirmations or visualise your goals.

Second, your reticular activating system cannot distinguish between events that really happen and ones that are created in our imagination. In other words, it accepts whatever message you give it. Imagine you're going to be giving a speech. You can practice giving that speech by visualising it in your mind. This 'pretend' practice will actually improve your ability to give the speech.

The Reticular Activating System is what I believe is the control mechanism for what is also known as "The Law of Attraction" (see Chapter 3). By controlling what the RAS filters out and what it draws our attention to, we can and will shape our lives by ensuring we see and act on the opportunities that come our way every day that will help us achieve our goals.

Motivation and Decision

What makes people choose to do something? What made you choose to pick up this book?

Some people believe in destiny or fate, that we are just kind of riding a train that can only go on its track in one direction, and it has few stops along the way until it reaches its destination.

I personally believe in decision – that we are like sailing boats and yes, we can let the wind carry us in any direction it pleases, but we can, at any time, decide to take control by moving the sails or even pulling the sails down and turning on the engine.

So what makes us decide? What makes us do anything?

There are two main motivating factors that influence every decision you make, and they are:

- Pleasure

- Pain

Pleasure and pain, two simple motivators.

Let me put it to you this way. If you're a woman, and you wake up in the morning, do you put on makeup because you love the process of putting on makeup? Or do you decide to put it on because, well, you'll feel more attractive, or maybe people will make mean comments if you're the only one not wearing makeup at the office today?

And if you are a man, do you shave because you love

There are $183 of Bonus Gifts Waiting for You...

shaving? Or is it because, just like the women, you get given compliments when you're cleanly shaven, or you feel more professional? Or maybe there's a dress code at your office and you'll be fired if you have unsightly facial hair.

In both of these examples, your decisions to put on makeup or to shave are completely based on two motivators – pleasure and pain.

So which one is the more powerful of the two? Is it pleasure or is it pain?

Well, to be honest, just like your learning style, it's completely different for everyone.

Some people move towards pleasure, while others move away from pain. Again, just like the learning, we all do a bit of both and, in fact, we switch it up depending on the situation.

Here's a great question to ask yourself.

What would you work harder to do?

Save $1,000, or stop someone from stealing $1,000 from you?

I'm guessing you are like 80% of the people I've asked that question to and you would put much more effort into stopping someone from stealing $1,000 from you. And that's alright. There is no wrong answer. It's the understanding of this concept that is important.

You see, you associate more pain with the prospect of someone stealing the $1,000 that you spent so much time and effort earning or saving than you do pleasure with the prospect of saving another $1,000.

Again, let's look at how we all differ. Let's look at my sister and me, as we were growing up, as an example.

Our parents would use the usual threats: "If you don't do such and such, you'll have to go to your room."

Well, I learnt early on that I found pleasure in getting things done when I wasn't asked. If I was left a list of chores to do, I would really get agitated. I hated doing them, and, more often than not, it wouldn't all get done.

On the other hand, my sister may have been told that morning, "If you don't get your list of chores done, you can't go out." All of a sudden, before you know it, the list has been done and she's out enjoying herself.

What is the difference here?

My sister is a moving-away-from personality, at least when it comes to household chores.

I am a moving-towards personality. I enjoyed the possibility of the amazement my parents would have and the compliments I would probably get for taking the initiative to get a bunch of chores done.

And this is still true to this day. I am, in general, much more motivated by possibility and the pleasure the future may hold than I am by getting things done or making a decision to avoid pain.

If you are a parent, I encourage you to look at your kids with this in mind. Test it out, and learn whether their dominant preference is moving towards pleasure or away from pain, because if you understand this, you can motivate them to do almost anything.

In fact, that is the secret to motivating people to do anything – find out what they have a higher preference for in the situation you want to motivate them in. If they like to avoid pain, then stir up the hurt. Point out all the bad things that could happen if they don't do what needs to be done, but don't only focus on the negatives. They still need to know that there is pleasure at the end of it by doing it. All you need to realise is that when there is a dominance of pain avoidance or pleasure seeking, that is what you need to emphasise. But you also still need to do the opposite to truly motivate someone. There should always be pleasure and pain in the equation to then amount to a decision.

Habits

Habits are something that we all have. Many of them are actions we take for granted and do without thinking. Sometimes, this can be helpful; other times, these habits can hold us back.

So what are habits and how do they form?

A habit is a learned ritual, an autopilot program that is set to run when triggered by an event of some kind.

One of the first habits you probably ever mastered was walking.

Can you imagine how much time we would waste every morning if we had to relearn how to walk? You see, as children, we practiced and practiced and did it over and over again until it became a habit. Our brains didn't have to think anymore. We just pressed "play" to run this program, and away we went. We were walking.

What about your journey to and from work? The first few times, you really had to think about where you were going and what time you had to be where. Now, you probably arrive at work and don't even really have much memory of the trip to work.

This is the essence of habits. Once you start on a familiar series of actions, you stop thinking about them, and you are able to complete them without conscious thought or attention.

A habit is a series of steps that have been learned gradually and sometimes without conscious awareness.

Habit formation is a type of procedural learning in which the basal ganglia, a cluster of nuclei located in the forebrain between the cortex and the brainstem, play a key role.

You see, this area of the brain provides access to both the frontal cognitive areas of decision making as well as the midbrain section, which controls your motor movement. It is actually the only place in the brain that deals with both physical and cognitive actions simultaneously, linking thoughts to movement.

Since a habit is a series of behaviours bound together and

There are $183 of Bonus Gifts Waiting for You...

then initiated by a particular event, understanding this can help you on your path to removing habits or creating new ones.

If you are creating a new habit, and you don't do the exact same thing, exactly the same every time you repeat the sequence, then you will find developing the habit is harder, as the neural connections aren't following the exact same path every time. Likewise, to stop a habit, it may be as simple as avoiding the first step in the series of steps, so then the path isn't even initiated.

Habits are key to our survival. If we had to think about walking, breathing or digesting, we would never have time to explore the more creative and inventive areas of our lives that have helped get the human race to where it is today.

By understanding the way we think, we now have the schematics and can let the builders get to work in making changes. They know exactly where to start working and how to ensure that the foundations stay strong.

Chapter Three

LEARNING THE CONTROLS

How thoughts affect the world we live in

> " *You become what you think*
> *about most of the time.*
>
> – Brian Tracy "

There are $183 of Bonus Gifts Waiting for You...

As you have just learnt, the brain is a complex and amazing thing; think about it. You see, that's the point. You can think about it. Your brain is what is letting you think about the fact that you actually have a brain and that it is what has helped you get to this point here in your life, that made you decide to pick up this book and read it to this paragraph.

The great thing to also realise is that there is only one thing in the world that you have 100% complete unequivocal control over.

And that, my friend, is the way you THINK.

Hasn't that gotten you excited? I mean, think about this for a moment...

No one, and I mean NO ONE, else can make you think anything – it's all you.

And the reason that is so exciting is that the way you think controls absolutely everything that you perceive about the world and how you approach every situation you are faced with.

That is the most exciting prospect of all because if YOU are the only person who controls how YOU think, then YOU have the power to perceive the world in exactly the way you want.

But let's look now for a moment at how our thoughts do affect the world around us as well as how the thoughts of others can affect our own.

The Law of Attraction

Have you noticed that sometimes when you need something to happen, everything just seems to fall into place or comes to you completely out of the blue?

Maybe you're thinking about someone or something, and then when you're walking through the shops, you bump into them or you see what you've been thinking about.

Perhaps you met your partner or your best friend just by the fate of being at the right place at the right time.

These scenarios are all evidence of what is known as the Law of Attraction.

Put simply, the law can be stated as follows:

I attract to my life what I give my energy, focus and attention to, whether positive or negative.

What this means is that your life right now and everything in it is the sum of all the thoughts you have had right up until this moment.

We live in a world of vibrations. Right down to a subatomic level, particles are vibrating. These vibrations are both positive and negative.

It's no different with your thoughts. Your thoughts have a vibration, and they can be positively or negatively charged.

The word "vibe" is often used as a way to describe a feeling or a mood. People get a bad vibe about a situation, and you pick up good vibes around certain people.

There are $183 of Bonus Gifts Waiting for You...

Each and every second, you are having a mood or a feeling, and it is either positive or negative.

And this is where the Law of Attraction comes in. The Law of Attraction is responding to your vibrations. Right now, the universe is matching the vibration you are giving off and giving it back.

Imagine this: It's Monday morning, and you've just woken up. You're feeling tired and a bit cranky. You think to yourself, "Arghh... work's a real pain. Why do I have to be there? Can't I just go back to bed?" You've just sent out negative vibrations.

And the Law of Attraction responds back, so on the way to work, you miss your bus, and then when you arrive, you find that the staff meeting has already started and you have to have a sit-down meeting with your boss to discuss your tardiness.

Or imagine this instead: You've just gotten off the phone with a great customer, and you're in a great mood. You're sending off positive vibrations. The phone rings again, and it's another customer telling you they want to place a large order. At the end of the day, you catch yourself saying, "It was one of those great days today."

The Law of Attraction has no bias towards you and is not concerned with what is fair or unfair. It is a balance of positive and negative.

If you focus on negatives, you will see only more negatives.

If you focus on positives, your life will be richly rewarded with positive outcomes.

The Influence of your Own Thoughts

As has been mentioned before, the one thing you have complete control of is the way you think, and these thoughts have a profound impact on how you view the world.

But have you ever actually stopped to think about your thoughts?

What are thoughts? Let's look at a simple breakdown.

There are $183 of Bonus Gifts Waiting for You...

Words

=

Thoughts
(made up of words)

=

Feelings
(positive or negative)

So, essentially, your thoughts are words that are just not said out loud. However, by saying things aloud, you are still thinking them just the same.

Positive thinking is contagious. People around you pick up on your mental moods and are affected accordingly. Think about happiness, good health and success and you will cause people to like you and desire to help you because they enjoy the vibrations that your positive mind emits.

But just as positive thinking is contagious, so is negative thinking. People around you will feel these negative thought vibrations, and they will not enjoy being around you. This will fuel more negative thoughts and create a spiral down into a depressed state.

Stop asking yourself what you don't want.

Ask yourself what you do want.

Here in Australia, there is a common Aussie slang expression that we all use:

"No worries."

When people thank us, we always say, "No Worries."

"No worries" has two negative concepts. Instead, when someone thanks you, try saying,

"You're welcome."

"My pleasure."

I guarantee you will start having people thank you a lot more.

Positive thinking is the key...

Think positively and expect only favourable results and situations, even if your current circumstances are not as you wish them to be. In time, your mental attitude will affect your life and circumstances and change them accordingly.

The Influence of Your Friends

How many times has someone said, "Don't forget" to you?

And what happened? Did you remember it or forget it?

Words – not only the words we speak but the words that others say to us or that we read – can have a profound impact on our thoughts. Notice that while words do have an impact on your thoughts, they do not control them.

When someone says to you, "Don't forget," the key word your brain hears is "forget," and it does exactly what it's been told to do – it forgets.

However, if your friend had said, "Remember to be at the station on time," your brain hears many positive commands. It knows it needs to remember to be at the station on time, rather than to forget.

But one of the most important and detrimental ways your friends can affect your thoughts is through their own doom and gloom and negativity.

How many times have you been out and someone has bitched about either someone else in the group or even a complete stranger?

How do you feel when they start this bitching? Do you jump in and become consumed by the feeling you get when you put others down? Or do you sit there and feel uncomfortable and notice that your general positive attitude is not as positive as it was before they started bitching?

Our friends impact us enormously, so here is the key. Share your knowledge with your friends, and help them learn the path of Kaizen and continuous self-improvement. Help them to learn positive thinking and the Law of Attraction.

But the really important thing to grasp is that you may, at some point, have to make new friends.

People can only change themselves. If they don't want to learn to think like you do and reap the rewards that such thinking brings, that is unfortunate and is their loss.

So often what is holding people back are the thoughts of their family, friends and others that are close to them. So get away from negative people. Certainly build up your strength of mind so that you can stay in a positive state while around these negative people. But the best way to stay positive is to minimise your exposure to negative situations.

I know it may seem hard to consider this right now, and I'm not saying you will have to do it. But if you accept that one day, your closest friends right now may no longer be people who are influencing your world in the way it needs to be influenced, then if the time comes, you will have no resistance, and it will just be a natural progression of change.

There is a story about a group of frogs that is a great example of how others influence us.

A group of frogs arranged a running competition. The goal was to reach the top of a very high tower. A crowd of frogs had all gathered around the tower to watch the race and cheer the contestants on.

So the race began... and the crowd started to talk.

"Oh, that tower is so high. They will NEVER make it to the top."

"Not a chance that they will succeed. It's too difficult."

The contestants, one by one, started collapsing.

There are $183 of Bonus Gifts Waiting for You...

The crowd kept shouting.

"It's too difficult!!! No one will make it to the top."

More and more of the frogs got tired and gave up...

But there was ONE little frog who continued higher and higher and higher.

This frog wouldn't give up!

At the end of the race, everyone else had given up on climbing the tower, except for the one tiny frog who, after a huge effort, was the only one who reached the top!

All the other contestants wanted to learn this frog's secret of how he reached the top of the tower.

As it turns out, this little frog was DEAF!!!

The wisdom that this story t e a c h e s is that you should never listen to other people's tendencies or allow them to project their beliefs onto you.

Be DEAF when people tell YOU that YOU cannot achieve YOUR dreams.

Always remember, "I CAN DO THIS!"

Asking the Right Questions and Listening to the Answers

Are you a member of the "If Only" club?

I would write that book if only...

I would grow that business if only...

If only... comes from asking the wrong question.

When you are asking the wrong questions, you get the wrong types of answers.

Let's look at some ineffective questions.

"What don't I want?"

"Can I fall back asleep again?"

"What difference will it make if I just skip my run today?"

Now, let's look at these same situations but with much more effective questions.

"What do I want?"

"What would be the best way to start my day?"

"Won't it feel great hitting the shower after my run?"

What's the difference?

The wrong questions are disempowering. They keep you focused on your own ego, your problems and your shortcomings. You are focusing on what's wrong, what isn't working. That might seem like a good idea, but as you have now been learning, your thoughts have a direct impact on the world around you, and these questions, whether asked internally or aloud are just as effective as, if not more effective than, your standard thoughts.

These wrong questions lead you to come up with answers that are useless and sometimes even destructive.

These wrong questions are quite sneaky, because they can become addictive. If you are feeling depressed, it may seem that the best question to ask yourself is, "Why am I so depressed?" Maybe you are thinking you can diagnose your problem and cure yourself. Unfortunately, it doesn't work that way. But what you can do is ask better questions!

The right questions are empowering. They keep you focused on solutions, on what you do have control of. Ultimately, the best way out of a negative situation is to think positively. The right type of thinking leads to action, while the wrong type of thinking sends you round in circles.

If you don't like the results you are getting, try asking better questions than the ones you usually ask.

Ask questions that turn your focus towards your goals instead of away from them. And remember to listen to the answers.

The Power of Decision

I've been told that back in the early seventies in America, there was a poster that read, "Not to decide is to decide."

So many people live in this state of indecision. You dream about the career you will have, the great relationships you will have, or the business you will start. But then you don't do it. You decide not to decide, and that actually becomes your decision.

Decide right now that your life will be different. Decide right now to do whatever it takes.

MAKE THE DECISION.

Decisions are extremely powerful. Once a decision is made, you can get past any excuses, any disbelief. Living in a state of indecision and having the decision made by default leaves you with an unsatisfying feeling. It creates a feeling of hope – hope that everything will turn out right. Hope then becomes your substitute for action.

Instead of getting up out of bed and making the world the way you want it to be, you sit in bed hoping that today will be better, that the perfect partner will just appear, instead of going out and meeting that person.

But by deciding that today you will make a change, that today you will meet someone, you will be motivated, you will be encouraged, and you will take action – because you have decided to.

Knowing vs. Hoping

"I think, therefore I am" – René Descartes

Certainty has a power about it. Have you ever met people who tell you their plans? They don't say, "Oh, I'd like to become an astronaut." They say, "I *will* become an astronaut." And you believe them! There isn't a doubt in your mind. Do you know why?

It's because they are saying it with 100% conviction and congruency. They completely and wholly believe that what they are saying is true. They KNOW they will achieve their goal.

There is a strong difference between HOPING and KNOWING.

Millions of people all around the world are hoping that their lives will change, that life can be better, that they will meet their perfect partner, or that they can become successful. So why aren't they all achieving it?

Because they are missing that gut feeling, that true, pure belief of knowing.

When you KNOW that you will achieve something, do you let people tell you that you can't do it?

When you KNOW that you will have success, do you give up at the first obstacle that comes along your path?

Absolutely not.

What about if you hope you will achieve something? Are

you likely to let someone convince you that you will never do it?

If you hope you will have success, and something gets in your way, are you likely to stick to it until that obstacle has been overcome?

The true power of KNOWING comes from having conviction and certainty, belief in oneself that there are no other options, that this is what will happen. And guess what? When you truly believe it, that there are no other options, well, then there are no other options. There is only one outcome possible, and that is success at achieving what you KNOW you will.

So you have now learnt a little more about how you think. You've learnt about the way your thoughts and the thoughts of others around you affect your life.

Do you think that by now having this understanding you can actually begin to shape the way you think and, in turn, your life?

Are you ready to get started on creating the life that you want and deserve?

Let's get into the next chapter and learn the secrets that people all over the world have been using to shape their lives exactly the way they want.

Chapter Four

WHAT MECHANICS KNOW
The science around it

"
Reality is merely an illusion,

albeit a persistent one

— Albert Einstein "

There are $183 of Bonus Gifts Waiting for You...

Disclaimer:

Before we get started, let me first clarify my position on this. In no way am I saying I fully understand or claim to be an expert in these sciences. However, my research and experience has shown that the following sciences do have relevance in our quest for Kaizen, and that many of the strategies and techniques I personally use have a strong foundation in these sciences.

Now that you understand that, know that we, as humans, primarily learn to be the way we are. Therefore, at any point in life, we can learn to be different. But, it may not be easy to change.

It is important to keep in mind that when your problems are severe and/or your self-help efforts are ineffective, you should seek professional help immediately.

The three main sciences from which the concepts in this book have been derived, and from which self-help practitioners and teachers all over the world have drawn their methods, techniques and strategies are:

- Neuro-linguistic Programming (NLP)

- Hypnosis

- Cognitive Behavioural Therapy (CBT)

In the next few pages, I will be discussing the history of these sciences (i.e., their foundations) and providing an overview of the techniques and applications of each science.

Let's begin...

Neuro-linguistic Programming (NLP)

Neuro-linguistic programming is an approach to explaining human behaviour, thought and communication through the modelling and understanding of thought patterns. It has also been known as the 'science of excellence.

The *Oxford English Dictionary* Draft Revision September 2009 states:

> "neurolinguistic programming n. a model of interpersonal communication chiefly concerned with the relationship between successful patterns of behaviour and the subjective experiences (esp. Patterns of thought) underlying them; a system of alternative therapy based on which seeks to educate people in self-awareness and effective communication, and to change their patterns of mental and emotional behaviour."

NLP was developed by Richard Bandler, a psychology student, and John Grinder, an assistant professor of linguistics, in the mid-1970s at the University of California, Santa Cruz. It was developed as a rapid form of psychological therapy, capable of addressing a full range of psychological problems such as phobias, depression, habit disorders, learning disorders and psychosomatic illnesses.

The principles of NLP are that there is a connection between Neurological processes ('Neuro'), language ('Linguistic') and behavioural patterns that have been learned through experience ('Programming').

NLP focuses on helping you to overcome your own self-perceived or subjective problems, rather than trying to diagnose or treat you for a mental or behavioural disorder.

While the main goals of NLP are therapeutic, the patterns have also been adapted for personal and professional use in communication and persuasion, including business communication, management training, sales, sports, and interpersonal influence.

Richard Bandler has come under fire from people who claim that he is touting that humans are like machines and that they can be programmed. However, Bandler has said that it is the opposite: "We are the only machine that can program itself."

Think about it. We have numerous programs running in the background on autopilot.

Here's a question – think about it:

When was the last time you thought about breathing? Or making your heart beat? What about blinking?

We do all of these on autopilot, yet we can use the focus of thoughts to take control of these autopilot programs, and we can override our breathing and blinking; some have been known to be able to slow down or even stop their heart beating for a short time.

You see, you don't think. Your body just does. It has these programs, and it executes them beautifully. With NLP, you learn to modify and create new programs that are just as automated.

For example, some of the techniques used in NLP to create these autopilot programs are:

- Visualisation

- Association

- Anchoring

- Framing

Let's discuss Anchoring for a moment.

The most famous example of anchoring is that of "Pavlov's Dog."

Ian Pavlov was a scientist who received the Nobel Prize in Physiology for his work on the mechanisms underlying the digestive system in mammals.

It was through this research with dogs that he discovered what he termed "conditioned reflexes." You see, reflexes are reactions that are programmed into us; they are these autopilot programs. For example, when a light beam hits our eyes, our pupils shrink in response to the light stimulus. The body responds in the same fashion every time the stimulus (the light) is applied.

This famous experiment involved Pavlov and his dogs. Pavlov's dogs were subjected to a series of experiments in which the built-in reflex of salivating just before eating food was linked or anchored to the sound of a bell.

There are $183 of Bonus Gifts Waiting for You...

Numerous times, as he fed his dogs, Pavlov would perform the ringing of a bell. He'd feed the dogs and ring the bell, feed the dogs and ring the bell.

Now the result of this experiment was that eventually, Pavlov stopped feeding the dogs when he rang the bell. He would just ring the bell. What do you think happened? The dogs salivated just as if they had been given food. They had learned a response. The salivation auto program was now anchored to the ringing of the bell.

This is how NLP Anchoring works. By conditioning responses to unique NLP anchors, we are able to deliberately get into specific states simply by triggering the unique NLP anchor, just like Pavlov's dogs.

The premise of setting NLP anchors is basically the same as that of Pavlov and his dogs. You set an NLP anchor by associating a unique trigger to a certain state or feeling. When in that state, trigger a unique anchor to associate the anchor with that state. After numerous repetitions, you can then just pull the trigger at any time to bring yourself into that state or feeling.

So to summarise, NLP is a field that builds models of human excellence and gives you direct strategies you can employ to help you on your path to Kaizen.

Hypnosis

Hypnosis is a mental state usually induced by a procedure known as hypnotic induction, which is commonly comprised of a series of preliminary instructions and suggestions.

You've seen the movies or been to the live shows. "You are feeling relaxed, deeply relaxed..." These common preliminary instructions and suggestions lead you into a hypnotic state.

Contrary to popular belief, hypnosis is not a form of unconsciousness or sleep. Research has shown that is actually a wakeful state of focused attention and heightened suggestibility.

It's a state of physical relaxation accompanied by mental concentration. In fact, it's quite similar to a meditative state.

The *Oxford English Dictionary* states:

> "hypnosis n. The induction of a state of consciousness in which a person loses the power of voluntary action and is highly responsive to suggestion or direction."

Modern hypnotherapy has been used in a variety of forms, such as regression hypnotherapy and Ericksonian hypnotherapy.

Applications of hypnosis include:

- Pain Management

- Weight Loss

- Quitting Smoking
- Skin Disease
- Soothing Anxiety
- Psychological Therapy
- Habit Control
- Relaxation
- Sports Performance

A number of studies have shown that hypnosis can reduce the pain experienced during burn wounds and childbirth.

There are few different types of hypnosis:

- Clinical Hypnosis
- Self-hypnosis
- Stage Hypnosis
- Covert Hypnosis

Clinical hypnosis involves going to see a hypnotherapist who directs you through the use of scripts and their knowledge to bring up old memories and reprogram limiting beliefs and other areas of your life.

Self-hypnosis occurs when a person hypnotises himself or herself, commonly involving the use of autosuggestion. The technique is often used to increase motivation for a particular goal or area of life you would like to improve.

Stage hypnosis is a form of entertainment traditionally done in clubs or theatres on a stage. Due to the artist's showmanship, many believe that hypnosis is a form of mind control. However, stage hypnosis is more about giving the subject an excuse to violate their own fear suppressors and the pressure to please the crowd. Those are the most common causes of the wild antics seen at hypnosis shows.

The plain fact is that hypnosis cannot force you to do anything you don't want to do. Hypnosis is purely a suggestion. You are in a state where you are much more open to these suggestions, but if you have a strong desire or problem with the suggestion you are being given, you will reject it.

Covert hypnosis is the ability to subtly communicate with another person's subconscious. It often takes place during regular conversation and is therefore also known as "conversational hypnosis."

There are $183 of Bonus Gifts Waiting for You...

The objective of covert hypnosis is to change the intended behaviour of the subject. An example would be a salesperson telling a customer how good she will feel buying the new product. Carefully selected words, body language and gestures can be intentionally used to convey the unspoken opinion and hypnotic suggestion.

But remember, they are only suggestions. The customer has the ability, if they feel strongly enough, to reject the suggestion.

Covert hypnosis and NLP are extremely similar and are often referenced together. Their techniques are also often used together.

A classic example of Covert Hypnosis...

"Right now, I want you to, whatever you do, not think about a big red ball. Do not see this big red ball bouncing along."

You saw a bouncing red ball didn't you?

That's because, to understand the sentence, your brain had to access your association of "red ball." I thereby induced a state in you through written communication just now.

Hypnosis, especially self-hypnosis and covert hypnosis, can greatly impact our journey to Kaizen, as we can use these techniques on ourselves to dramatically change how we think and react to situations.

Cognitive Behavioural Therapy (CBT)

Cognitive Behavioural Therapy is a psychotherapeutic approach that aims to solve problems concerning dysfunctional emotions, behaviours and cognitions through a goal-oriented systematic procedure.

There is powerful evidence that CBT is effective in treating a variety of problems, including:

- Moods

- Anxiety

- Personality

- Eating

- Substance Abuse

- Psychotic Disorders

CBT was primarily developed through a merging of behavioural therapy with cognitive therapy. While these two therapies are quite different in terms of fundamentals, they share a common ground in terms of focusing on the "here and now" and on alleviating symptoms.

The *Oxford English Dictionary* states:

"cognitive therapy n. a type of psychotherapy in which negative patterns of thought about the self and the world are challenged."

There are many different techniques and they vary within the different approaches.

Some common CBT techniques are as follows:

- Keeping a diary of significant events and associated feelings, thoughts and behaviours

- Questioning and testing cognitions, assumptions and beliefs that might be unhelpful and unrealistic

- Gradually facing activities that you may have been avoiding

- Trying out new ways of behaving or reacting to situations

CBT has been used effectively in mood control, since research has shown that depressed people have views like:

"I never do a good job."

"It is impossible to have a good day."

"Things will never get better."

These thoughts create a negative schema, which then creates a cognitive bias. This cognitive bias helps fuels the negative schema, which means depressed people have a negative outlook on all aspects of their life. It's a terrible and vicious cycle that continues to fuel itself.

A CBT approach to this would be the ABC model.

The ABC model asks you to record a sequence of events in terms of:

A – Activating Events (also sometimes described as triggers)

B – Beliefs (for example, the thoughts that occur to you when the activating event happens)

C – Consequences (how you feel and behave when you have those beliefs)

Here's an example:

A - Activating	B - Belief	C - Consequences
My co-worker asks if I have completed a piece of work.	I think: "They don't think I am working hard enough" "They want to take my job by catching me out"	I defensively say that I've nearly finished, although I'm not anywhere near finished. And I feel angry, annoyed and resentful

By writing this out, you can clearly see what triggered your belief that caused you to react either in action or in thoughts or emotions.

By understanding this, you can then counteract it, seeing the beliefs you need to address and thinking of better ways you could have reacted.

So in the above example, you could then use balancing statements.

"It is possible they don't think I'm working hard enough, but it is also possible they are enquiring to see if they can help in any way, or just to ensure I remember that the deadline is approaching and there is nothing personal about it."

CBT, in a nutshell, is about making sensible assessments of your situation and making the most constructive choices

There are $183 of Bonus Gifts Waiting for You...

that you can to improve or cope with that situation.

The human mind is an amazing biological and electrical machine, and science is continually making new and astounding discoveries. But we have already found that there is strong evidence to show that direct techniques can be used to control our world just by controlling our thoughts.

Chapter Five

DRIVER'S HANDBOOK

How to create the life you want and deserve

" *Happiness is not something readymade. It comes from your*

own actions.

– Dalai Lama "

There are $183 of Bonus Gifts Waiting for You...

Now it's time. You've learnt the background; you understand the why and the how. So, what next?

It's time to create that life you want and deserve, learn the process that you can use and put into action to attract into your life everything you have ever and will ever want.

Life is for the taking, so let's take it!

What Right Do You Have?

A common limiting belief is the belief that you have no right to have everything you ever wanted in life. There is a guilt that because others are not living their lives in abundance, neither should you.

I'm here to tell you, that's rubbish. You have every right to be as successful, happy, fulfilled and abundant as you want and rightly deserve to be.

Another great saying I take to heart that has relevance here is this:

"Why create mediocrity, when you can model genius?"

Just because others are living mediocre lives, doesn't mean you have to. There are plenty of people who are successful, who are living happy and fulfilled lives, and you have just as much right to be like them as the people who decide to live in mediocrity.

A question that has been asked of me a few times when I have mentioned my long-term vision of the future is this:

"Why should you be rich when there are people starving

all around the world?"

And believe me, I think it is a valid question. But the people who ask me this are missing the point.

Yes, unfortunately, there are people who have been born into circumstances that are challenging. Yes, you and I have been blessed to not have such a challenge in our upbringing. Now here's the but...

Let's say I decided that instead of living a happy, successful and financially free life, I would live an average life, where I worried about paying my bills and had to focus on getting by in life. If I were to make that choice, how many of those starving people would I be helping?

Now if I were someone who didn't have to worry about paying my bills, who didn't have to swap my time for money in a job, and whose mind wasn't always focusing on myself and my own troubles, how many of those starving people or other countless charities and things could I be helping?

You see, I don't disagree with these people one bit, but you need to remember, they just aren't thinking the way you and I do.

You need to decide that you have the right – in fact, I could even say the DUTY – to be the best that you can possibly be. Because as you become a better person, you will create a more fulfilled life and you will be able to give more back to society and the world.

There are $183 of Bonus Gifts Waiting for You...

So What's the Big Secret?

Let's look at one of the biggest breakthroughs in the history of invention:

The wheel

No one can say for sure exactly who invented the wheel or when the wheel was invented, but according to archaeologists, it was probably invented around 8,000 BC in Asia. It was invented through various stages of trial and error and perfection.

It started in the early stages as a large trunk from a tree being cut down and placed as a roller underneath large and heavy objects to help them be moved around.

The wheel was further improved on later by the Egyptians, who made wheels with spokes, which were used in the Egyptian chariots of around 2,000 BC. Later still, the Roman Empire engaged in wheel-making and produced a great variety of wheeled vehicles.

Today, we see that the wheel has indeed undergone many changes, but the fundamental lessons were learned very early on, and the knowledge passed on – in fact, human progress in general – was built on collective knowledge. Someone learned some lessons and documented these lessons so that others didn't have to learn them all over again through trial and error. It speeds up invention and progress.

Do you think that if we still had to work out the concept of the wheel, we, the human race, would be where we are today?

The secrets of success, happiness and a life of fulfilment are no different from this basic concept of the wheel.

The trick is to use collective knowledge to speed up your progress.

1. Know what you want.

2. Find others who have what you want.

3. Learn how they got it.

4. Find a path used that you connect with.

5. And do as they did.

Model other people's successes. Don't keep reinventing the wheel. There is no need, and you waste precious time.

Did you know that there are 4,217.2 weeks in the average lifespan?

There are $183 of Bonus Gifts Waiting for You...

How many of these weeks have you used up already?

Do you want to reach your ultimate life as quickly as possible, or do you want to go through at a snail's pace?

The universe works by cause and effect. What you want to achieve is the effect. All you need to know is how this effect is caused.

This is where you find others who have done as you wish to do and learn what they did. Now you have a clear cause that, if replicated, should create the same effect.

They have made mistakes. They have learnt lessons along the way. So skip these mistakes. Don't make them all over again. Learn the lessons of those that have come before you and achieve your desires much more rapidly.

Let's put it another way: Thomas Edison discovered 3,000 different ways to not create a light bulb before he managed to find one way to create it.

When the light bulb went into mass production, do you think they had to go through all those thousands of non-working designs before they had a working light bulb? Absolutely not. They had the schematics. They had notes on some of the intricacies and troubles that could come up, and they produced the light bulb.

The Process

Ok, so the fundamentals are now obvious.

$$\text{Causes} \rightarrow \text{Effects.}$$

Let's go a little deeper into a process that you can follow that will help you in creating your roadmap to your ultimate destination.

Step out of Time

Let us begin by taking a step out of time for a moment. I want you to imagine that you have just stepped out of your life as it is right now and come through what seems to be a big TV. You have a remote control in your hand; you can pause, rewind and fast-forward everything on the screen. What you see on the screen is your life.

There are $183 of Bonus Gifts Waiting for You...

Why are we here? Because before making any good plans for the future, it's important to understand where we have been and where we are now.

So the first step in the process is looking in the rear-view mirror.

What are the three main significant events that have shaped your life up to this point in time? Are there more than three? How did they shape you?

Did they have a positive impact or a negative impact?

What lessons have you learnt on your journey to date? Have you repeatedly learnt these lessons and expected different results?

Your past is an important part of your life. Everything – and I mean every single thought, event, person you have met and book you have read – has shaped your personality and life to date. Throughout these events, you have learnt lessons. Maybe you learnt that mixing your milo into the ice cream makes it so much better, or that touching the oven when it's on is not a good idea, or that respecting others is of paramount importance. These lessons are important and should always be remembered.

Now remembering the lessons from the past is healthy, but being consumed by past events and not letting go is not. You must learn to put the past just as it is, behind you. Sure, recall it, learn the lesson, but then move on. Live here in the present.

So here in the present, what do we need to know? We need

to know that we are in control. That's why you and I are here having this conversation. You are ready to learn to be in control. You need to know in what direction to steer the boat of your life, and to do that, we need to look now into the future.

The future consists of your goals. Where do you plan to be? Don't worry about the how you are going to get there yet. Remember, you just need to know which direction to head in when you are back in the present. You don't need to know about the weather conditions just yet.

Now it's time to hit "play" on the remote control and step back into the real world. You've stepped out of time just long enough to learn your past lessons, set a clear course and head off towards the future.

Turning Dreams into Reality

A four-step process is used to turn your dreams into reality. I call this process the M.I.C.A. Principle. These four steps are simple in nature and yet very powerful when you follow them.

The M.I.C.A. Principle is as follows:

1. Mentality

2. Imagination

3. Commitment

4. Action

There are $183 of Bonus Gifts Waiting for You...

Mentality

You have already learnt a lot about this concept in previous chapters. This is the process of getting your mind clear and ready to accept your dreams as reality.

It is the first step because without clarity of mind, all the other steps fall away.

You must accept that you WILL HAVE all that you desire, that you are an extraordinary person who has complete control of your life.

You must learn to think big and stretch possibilities as far as you can. No longer are you a short-term, small thinker.

Imagination

A picture is worth a thousand words. That's what they say. And as discussed earlier, your brain can't distinguish between reality and fantasy, so your imagination and visualisations are powerful tools when turning your dreams into reality.

In this second step, you must begin to train your subconscious using visualisation. Picture yourself living the life of your dreams as if you have already achieved it.

Use meditation and visual stimuli daily to keep it fresh.

Commitment

If you haven't told anyone your plans, how committed to them are you really?

Who are you accountable to? Who's going to keep you in check?

This third step is crucial. You must hold yourself accountable (and have others hold you accountable as well) for your actions and your goals.

Use affirmations and "I am" statements. Say them with emotional conviction. Repeat them to yourself every day, and tell your friends, family and strangers your goals and your plans. The more people you tell, the more compelled you will be to live up to what you have said.

Action

You've planted the seeds in the previous three stages. It's now time to kick it up a notch and get yourself hungry and emotional for this reality.

Take action on your goals and dreams. If your dream is to own a million-dollar yacht, then go out and learn to drive a boat.

If you would like to be an Olympic swimmer, attend the Olympics and see all the swimming events you can.

Get yourself hungry. Give your mind the taste of achievement.

As you become hungrier and more motivated towards your goal, you will notice and do more things that move you closer to this goal. It will just occur subconsciously if you have followed the M.I.C.A. Principle.

This M.I.C.A. Principle is not just a do-it-once system. It is an ongoing and continuous loop. You must be in all four stages all the time, except for when you first start out.

There are $183 of Bonus Gifts Waiting for You...

That is the only time you must start at mentality and move through the steps to action. Once you have made it to action, you will be using all four stages simultaneously for amazing success.

The Five Areas of Improvement

There are five main areas that most people focus on throughout their Kaizen journey.

These areas are:

1. Body and Health

2. Finances

3. Relationships

4. Recreation

5. Work

Body and Health

Good health is more precious than gold.

Your physical body and general health are vitally important. Think about this – without health, how will you enjoy all the other parts of your life?

Achieving good health is an ongoing process of maintenance. It is true Kaizen. So what are the areas you should focus on?

The four areas of health that I recommend you focus on are:

- Nutrition

- Physical Activity and Exercise

- Stress Management

- Sleep

Finances

Financial freedom and not being tied to the stress of money will not only allow you to have all the material objects and the lifestyle that you desire, but it will also allow you to give back to the world, be it through angel investments or through donations to charities.

It is no secret that money opens up doors and knocks down walls.

The areas of finance that I recommend you focus on are the following:

- Financial Position (Net worth and cash flow)

- Adequate Protection (Insurance)

- Tax Planning (Never pay more tax than you legally have to)

- Investments (How will you accumulate money?)

- Estate Planning (When you die, what happens to your finances?)

Relationships

Relationships with friends, Relationships with family, Relationships with strangers, Relationships with Partners...

Human beings need relationships. We are creatures of community. We enjoy company. It is your duty to have amazing relationships with everyone you possibly can. Relationships are about giving and taking. Don't be only a giver and don't be only a taker. Learn to balance.

The areas of relationships are:

- Close Personal Friends
- Intimate Relationships
- Family Relationships
- Business Relationships

Recreation

Life is fun; enjoy it. Don't take it so seriously. Get out and about. Have hobbies and do activities.

Work

Whether you choose to be a successful entrepreneur, the best chef in the country, the world's most productive personal assistant, or a generous philanthropist, you should strive to be at the top of your field or area of work.

Work, for some people, involves going to a job. For others, it involves not having to go to a job. But to keep your mind active and healthy, you should have something that you do on a regular/semi-regular basis that you would call work.

When working on these areas, the biggest key is education. The more you know about the different areas, your options, and how to be more effective, the better you will become in all these areas.

Creating the life you desire is not something only few can achieve. Anyone can do it. It's just up to you. If you follow these principles and teachings, you will see dramatic changes in the way you view the world, your life and the relationships you have with the great people you share your world with.

Chapter Six

Set the GPS Navigation

Ensure you reach your ultimate destination

" *If what you're doing is not moving you towards your goals, then it's moving you*

away from your goals

— Brian Tracy "

It's time to think about your specific roadmap, how you will reach your destination of the life you've dreamed of.

This roadmap is made up of goals.

Goals vs. Dreams

So what is the difference between a goal and a dream?

I believe there is only one main component that marks the difference between them, and that is time frame.

Dream + Time frame = Goal

A dream has no time frame. Once you add a time frame to it, it has become a goal – not necessarily a SMART goal, which we will get into shortly, but a goal just the same.

You see, goals are targets that can be aimed at, the steps, if you will, that take us to our dreams, while dreams are the bigger pictures that the goals work towards.

How to Set Goals that You Will Achieve

Setting goals is more than just deciding what you want to do. It involves figuring out what you need to do to get where you want to go, and how long it will take you to get there.

This is done by applying the principles of SMART when you are setting goals.

Every time you set a goal, ask yourself if it is a SMART goal.

SMART stands for

    S = Specific

    M = Measureable

    A = Achievable

    R = Realistic

    T = Time frame

Specific

Goals should be straightforward and emphasize what you want to happen.

Specifics help us to focus and clearly define what we are going to do.

Ask yourself the following:

What, Why and How?

What am I trying to do?

Why is this important for me to do this at this time?

How am I going to do it?

There are $183 of Bonus Gifts Waiting for You...

Measurable

If you can't measure it, how will you know you're getting anywhere?

Measurements should be made through some form of unit. This may be in the form of time (in minutes, hours, months, or weeks,), weight (in kilograms or grams), etc.

Let's look at an example for a moment.

"I want to get fit."

Is this goal measureable? No, it's not.

"I want to complete a 10-k run in under one hour by December 12."

Is this still the same goal? Absolutely, since to be able to do that, you need to be fit. Is it 100% measureable?

You can track your progress against the time as well as the distance.

Achievable

How achievable is your goal?

Have others done it before you?

What past experiences of your own or of others can you use to show that it's achievable?

For example, if your goal was to lose 5 kg in 2 weeks and you had, in the past, lost 2.5 kg in only 1 week, you know that 5 kg in 2 weeks should be achievable.

Realistic

Let's clarify something here. Realistic doesn't equal "easy."

Realistic is more of a question of "is it doable for you?"

For example, if your goal is to be an Olympic swimmer in 2 years, yet at this moment, you do not know how to swim, it may not be a realistic goal for you.

You need to devise a plan that will make it realistic for you, and sometimes it just means a change of specifics.

For example:

If your goal was to eat only one piece of junk food per day, you may find that looking at the specifics might help with making it realistic.

If we changed the goal to focus on eating one piece of fruit per day rather than one piece of chocolate, we are still aiming at the same fundamental goal of health. But it may make it a more realistic goal for you to achieve and keep you motivated to continue working at it.

Time Frame

If you were catching a train somewhere, would you just show up at the train station on any day without knowing when your train was arriving or leaving?

Without an end point in time, your target is open-ended and any urgency is lost.

It's too vague, and you tend to get nowhere because you feel you can start at any time, whereas with a time frame,

There are $183 of Bonus Gifts Waiting for You...

as that end point gets closer, if you haven't started on your goal, the urgency will kick in and you will just have to dive right in.

Remember, when setting a time frame, it too must adhere to the other principles of SMART.

The time frame should be specific, measureable, achievable and realistic.

A great way to ensure it meets these criteria is to set a very specific time, even down to the day, month and hour.

The Hierarchy of Goals

If you do one task every day, how can you not achieve your goal?

There is a hierarchy to goal setting, a process of breaking down goals into smaller goals. Why do we do this? Have you ever heard the old adage, "How do you eat an elephant? One bite at a time."? This is very relevant to goal setting.

Often what stops us from achieving goals is the fact that we don't start, and usually not starting is due to procrastination

There are $183 of Bonus Gifts Waiting for You...

because of the sheer amount of work required to achieve most long-term goals.

So we break them down. We start with our dreams. As discussed, usually the simplest way to set a long-term goal is to add a time frame to your dream. Then, of course, apply the principles of SMART to bring it into line.

Now look at that long-term goal and break it down into smaller steps. These become your mid-term goals.

Again, these mid-term goals need to be broken down into short-term goals. Then the short-term goals are broken down into tasks.

Tasks are a bit different from goals. They are small, actionable steps that can be done very quickly. For example, a short-term goal may be to apply for a loan to buy a property, and a task for that would be to meet with a mortgage broker. Another task would be to sign the paperwork. These are all quick and simple tasks that should take no longer than two days at most to complete.

Sometimes I have found that tasks just aren't specific and simple enough, and I actually have to go to subtasks, but this is not a common scenario for me. However, you can use subtasks if required to make the goal more manageable.

Timescale for the Different Goals

Tasks = small, achievable steps, 2 days at most to complete

Short-term Goals = 1 – 12 months

Mid-term Goals = 2 – 5 years

Long-term Goals = 5+ years

Task Lists

Are you a lover or a hater of lists? It's interesting, actually, as everyone is so diverse. I know people who absolutely love lists. Everything is in lists. But then there are others who are sent into a brain freeze and shut down at the mere thought of lists.

I personally find task lists empowering, and that is why I am an avid advocator of using them with your goals.

As you have learnt from the goal hierarchy, once you have broken your short-term goals down into tasks, and sometimes even into subtasks, you have a massive list of things to do. So what do you do with it?

Start using daily, weekly and/or monthly lists.

Take this massive list of all the tasks you need to complete to achieve your goals, and start working away at them.

Every day, have at least one task, just one task per day. And that means each and every day of your life, you will be moving one step closer to achieving your goals.

If you haven't already, I want you to think back to some of your past goals that you didn't achieve. Are they still relevant? Do you still want to achieve them?

Where do they fit in the hierarchy of goals? Why didn't you achieve them? Were they SMART?

Starting off by reworking old goals is a great way to practice these new goal-setting strategies, so go on, give it a try and always achieve the goals you set yourself by following these principles.

Chapter Seven

DON'T STOP AT TRAFFIC LIGHTS

What holds us back

> *If you always do what you've always done, you'll always get*
>
> *what you've always got*
>
> – Unknown

Why is it that we get so enthused about something, we seem to be committed, but then nothing happens? Our goals never seem to be reached. We just seem to give up.

What are the things that hold us back and stop us from achieving the great things we are all capable of?

You see, if it were easy to achieve great things, everyone would have done it. Life likes to put up challenges along the way to test us and ensure we are worthy of our prize.

Success is simple, but not necessarily easy.

Fear

One of the most common obstacles that gets in the way of our plans each and every day is FEAR.

Fear is that feeling you get, those "what if" questions, that tickle in the back of your throat.

Would you like to learn how to look at fear in a completely new light? To be able to go, "Yes, I understand that fear, and I choose to overcome it"?

Let's look at the standard definition of fear.

The *Oxford English Dictionary* states:

> "fear n. 1. an unpleasant emotion caused by the threat of danger, pain, or harm 2. the likelihood of something unwelcome happening."

Emotions play an important part in our daily lives. And the fear response is one of those emotions. It is a pre-programmed emotion that is found in all animals and people, an instinctual response to potential danger.

When you experience fear, certain areas in your brain are immediately activated and begin to control some of your physical responses.

Some of the following are the most common fear responses:

- Rapid Heart Rate

- Increased Blood Pressure

- Tightening of Muscles

- Sharpened or Redirected Senses

- Dilation of the Pupils

- Increased Sweating

But is fear truly instinctual or is it learned?

There are certain types of fears that are truly instinctual – fears that trigger the Fight or Flight response. For example, if you were being mugged in a dark alleyway and the mugger pulled a knife or a gun on you, the fear you would feel would be instinctual. It would not just be your irrational thoughts.

But there are many fears that we have learnt; these fears are irrational and get in the way of our progress towards Kaizen.

Let's look more closely at what these learned fears really are.

There are $183 of Bonus Gifts Waiting for You...

Fear consists of thoughts in your head. They are thoughts of the future, based upon what we have experienced in the past and what we think is going to happen in the future.

Not all fear is always bad, however. A small amount of fear before an important speech actually has a biological purpose. It encourages you to focus on your thoughts and avoid getting sidetracked. But so often the fear response for many goes into overload and actually detracts from its purpose of focus, causing people to freeze and forget their thoughts. This overload of fear is what we must learn to control, and, like all of my favourite re-education processes, using an acronym is the best way to learn it.

Let's take the word "fear" and dissect it into two acronyms that you can remember and recall whenever you feel fear. That will allow you to bring yourself back under control and back to a useful level of fear response.

F = False

E = Expectations

A = Appearing

R = Real

But that isn't all. Let's look further.

F = Finding

E = Excuses

A = And

R = Reasons

To Claim Them visit www.KaizenSeries.com/RMG

So what have you learnt?

Fear is nothing more than your mind finding False Expectations that Appear Real and then Finding Excuses And Reasons to avoid the situation.

Does that make you feel uplifted? Does having this new definition of fear give you greater control?

If you understand that fear is completely in your mind and that, while your mind might have very convincing evidence, you can often overcome it by just asking better questions.

For example:

I used to be petrified of heights. I would feel like I would fall and I couldn't go near an edge.

How do I continually face this fear?

I ask myself this question:

"Has anyone ever fallen from doing this without doing something idiotic?"

Asking yourself questions is a powerful way to overcome limiting beliefs and fears. You see, by asking the right questions, you can completely blow all that false evidence out of the water and prove to yourself that it is false. And you then remember this definition – that you are just finding excuses and reasons.

There are $183 of Bonus Gifts Waiting for You...

Bad Habits

Maybe you have always done something so often that it's a habit. But is that habit benefiting you or holding you back?

Scientists have come up with a host of reasons why humans stick to habits that they actually know are bad.

For example, most smokers I speak to know that their habit of smoking is bad for their health and the health of others around them, but they do not try to stop their habit. Why?

Among the reasons that scientists have found are:

- Innate human defiance
- Need for social acceptance
- Inability to truly understand the nature of risk
- Individualistic view of the world and the ability to rationalize unhealthy habits
- Genetic predisposition to addiction

Now, if you are one of these people who know they have bad habits but don't want to do anything about them, you are probably thinking, "Great, I now have five scientific reasons I can spout off as to why I won't change." WRONG!

You picked up this book for a reason, and you have read this far because you have committed to a life of Kaizen and you know that it is your right and duty to be a better person, so don't let these excuses become acceptable.

Bad habits, addiction and healthy habits are all subconscious behaviours that have been formed through repetition. And as was discussed back in Chapter 2, these habits are just neural pathways that are being triggered.

So what does that mean? It means that these habits can be changed, or skipped.

It takes about 21 days of determination and discipline to change or form a new habit. Some habits, however, are so ingrained, so deeply and so often performed, that the brain will take a little longer to overcome them.

So would you like a structured approach you can follow to assist you in breaking your bad habits?

The process is as follows:

- Identify the Trigger

- Ask Yourself, "Why?"

- Commit to the Benefit

- Repeat the New Process

So you must start by identifying the trigger.

You don't overeat, smoke or carry out your behaviour all the time. Something triggers you to start the autopilot program in your brain to follow a particular pathway.

So the next time you feel that urge to act out your bad habit, pause, become of aware of it, and try to identify what it is that is triggering this sequence.

Next, you must ask yourself, "Why?" This is done by

There are $183 of Bonus Gifts Waiting for You...

communicating with yourself so that you can look for the underlying intention.

Ask yourself what you are trying to gain by doing this behaviour. Search for the answer from your unconscious. Listen carefully because your mind will come up with many answers.

You need to find the inner motivation that is causing you to repeat this undesirable pattern.

Ask yourself this:

"If I continue doing (insert your habit here), what do I perceive that I will gain?"

By learning what the underlying motivation is, sometimes just realising that you have no true reason for doing it is enough to help you completely overcome the habit.

You must also commit to the benefit that removing this habit will bring. You can't just say, "Well, I'd like to change my habit." Why do you want to change? What will it mean to you and your life?

Realise this, and commit to that new benefit and reason for change.

Now comes the most challenging part – repeating the new process.

To remove a habit, you must either create a new one or completely override the existing habit. And that is done through repetition.

You must make a conscious effort to see your new image and act out, in a regular, consistent sequence, a new process that brings about a desirable result rather than an undesirable one.

Do you really want to change?

Many people complain about something even if they don't really want to change it.

In fact, complaining is often a way to release stress. You complain about the situation, but then you accept it even though you don't particularly like it.

So ask yourself this: Have you really decided to change?

If the answer is no, praise yourself right now for having the courage and the insight to actually admit to yourself that this is the case.

On the other hand, if you really do want to change and you are ready, the next question to ask yourself is...

Is now the right time?

When changing a habit, it's important to focus on one habit change at a time. So if your plate is extremely full right now, you may want to wait before introducing the new challenge of changing a habit.

Successful habit change requires strong motivation, and if now isn't the right time, you may find that keeping that motivation is challenging.

There are $183 of Bonus Gifts Waiting for You...

A great way to keep you motivated through your time of habit change is to draw up a two-column sheet on the habit as follows.

Pleasure I Will Gain	Pain I Will Avoid

Do you remember back in Chapter 2 when we spoke about motivation and how we make decisions? Pleasure and pain are the two things that we use to determine everything.

So write up all the pleasures you will gain by replacing this habit with your new habit and all the painful things you will no longer experience once the habit is gone. Put this up on your wall or next to your mirror, and every day, it will firstly, remind you to change this habit, and secondly, keep you motivated as to why you are making this change and what it will mean for you.

In addition to having these strong commitments of the pleasures and pains associated with this new habit, you also need to direct strong energy toward your behaviour.

Learn to hate your bad habit. Learn to love yourself and your desire to change. Commit to this new habit and the removal of the old one by telling friends, family, even strangers if you choose to. The more people you tell, the more committed you will become.

So what happens when you backslide on your habits? That's ok. You need to remember, we are human. We aren't perfect. If we were, then we would have no need for a Kaizen attitude. The important thing to do when you backslide is to give yourself the chance to redeem yourself.

Correct the habit, get back on track and start again. Winston Churchill once said, "Success is going from failure to failure without losing your enthusiasm." And what that means is that as long as you remember why you were making the change and don't give up, success is the only option left.

Knowing When It's Time to Quit

It's not fun to think about quitting. It's not the kind of thing that gets you motivated and wanting to read on, but I encourage you to learn why knowing when to quit and when not to is important.

It's a strange concept for most of us. Why would we quit something if we have decided that this is what we are going to do?

We have been predisposed to believe that quitting is bad. And I do agree with this, but not in its entirety. Let me explain...

Strategic quitting is a conscious decision; failing is when you give up on your dream.

There are $183 of Bonus Gifts Waiting for You...

Being smart and quitting a process that is no longer working is a great way to avoid failure. Let's think about it for a moment...

Your dream is to become a millionaire. You've opened a business as a florist as your path to this dream. The unthinkable happens. A disease spreads through your shop and kills all your plants and flowers. You've just lost hundreds of thousands of dollars, and you don't know what to do.

You have three options: You can cut your losses, close the business down and sell the assets to cap the costs right then and there; you can decide to cope, stick it out, and see what happens; or you can get really enthused and energised at this opportunity for change and business growth and take the business to the next level.

Now is coping with a situation really what you want to do? When we begin to cope with a situation, we are really starting to become mediocre.

Do you want to be mediocre or do you want to be the best?

So if you have lost your enthusiasm and can't seem to get it back, the strategic decision would be to quit, to close the business down and cut the losses.

You see, the end goal is not what you are quitting, but the process that you have chosen to take to get there.

If you have it clearly defined and are 100% committed to a goal, you won't be quitting achieving it at all, but what I'd like you to realise is that sometimes you will get to a point where what you are doing to get there is no longer working, and you have to make a choice.

You can continue trying and eventually break through this invisible ceiling, or you can change your approach.

A great analogy I was once told at a seminar is this...

If you can't get in through the front door, you try the back door, and if you can't get in through the back door, you open a window.

It is important to not just quit when things get tough. Life is full of challenges. It's not meant to be easy.

So how do you know when it's time to quit?

If you are considering quitting, ask yourself the following questions.

"Am I panicking? Is this only a momentary feeling?"

"Who does quitting benefit? Is it benefiting many people or only one?"

"What is my progress to date in this endeavour?"

If you are just panicking and making a decision in the heat

There are $183 of Bonus Gifts Waiting for You...

of the moment and height of your emotional state, then you are not going to be making a truly strategic decision.

If quitting is only benefiting one person, then it may be prudent to ask yourself how many people would benefit if you did not quit.

And your progress can only have three possible options. You're either progressing forward, standing still or falling backwards.

If you aren't progressing forward, then it's highly likely it's time to quit.

Comfort Zone

Comfort zones keep us doing the same old things, the way we've always done them.

And we all have them; it doesn't matter if you are student in school, a CEO of a large company, an athlete or a professional performer. No matter who you are or what you do, you have a comfort zone.

Your comfort zone is shaped by your experiences and what you know, so while all these different types of people have comfort zones, some are larger than others and contain different things.

Something a professional performer may have in their comfort zone won't necessarily be in a student's. On the other hand, that performer may find something that the student finds comfortable to be very uncomfortable.

Stepping out of your comfort zone causes your anxiety level

to rise. But the result of this anxiety is a stress response of enhanced concentration and focus. It's when we step out of this comfort zone that our biggest growth and learning take place.

So let's take a look at the Zones of Comfort.

COMFORT
ZONE

LEARNING ZONE

ANXIETY ZONE

There are three zones of comfort.

1. The Comfort Zone

2. The Learning Zone

3. The Anxiety Zone

Your Comfort Zone is full of everything you know. It is low-stress and where we like to stay.

There are $183 of Bonus Gifts Waiting for You...

Your Comfort Zone is:

- Normal

- Old

- Constant

- Safe

- Secure

- Low-stress

- Conformist

- Related to Past Successes

- Familiar

- Related to Stagnation and Mediocrity

- Comfortable

- Complacent

Your Learning Zone is where your anxiety level rises slightly, so you are in a peak state of learning. It's where you meet new people and do things that you know you don't like doing. And through doing these things, you learn and grow as a person.

Your Learning Zone is:

- Unknown

- New

- Transitional

- Knowledge-building

- Related to Risks and Mistakes

- Moderately Stressful

- Related to a Temporary Loss of Security

- Related to Change

- Non-Conformist

- Related to Future Successes

- Related to New Skills

- Fear-inducing

- Challenging

The final zone is your Anxiety Zone. This is where too many people throw themselves when they move out of their comfort zone. It's too far, too soon. It's where very little learning and growth actually occur.

Your Anxiety Zone is:

- Not Conducive to Learning

- Highly Stressful

- Likely to Render You Immobile

- Likely to Block Your Mind

To learn, you need to expand your horizons outside of your comfort zone and into the learning zone.

You must stretch into the learning zone far enough that

There are $183 of Bonus Gifts Waiting for You...

you will achieve growth and your goals, but your must be careful to not stretch yourself so far that you hit the anxiety zone.

If you project yourself into the anxiety zone, you will be learning very little and you will struggle to push yourself out of your comfort zone in the future due to the experience you felt whilst in the anxiety zone.

Your comfort zone is in either one of three states.

1. Steady

2. Growth

3. Retraction

If your comfort zone is in a steady state, you are stagnant. You need to start pushing yourself out into your learning zone and building your knowledge and experiences.

If it's growing, then you have moved into your learning zone and expanded your knowledge and experience in certain areas and tasks. Ideally, this is where you always want to be – in a state of growth.

Retraction occurs when maybe you have skipped doing something you used to be quite comfortable doing for so long. It comes time to do it again, and you no longer find it comfortable. Fear comes over you, and your anxiety levels rise.

This means your comfort zone has actually become smaller. It hasn't remained stagnant or grown. If you are at this stage, it's time for some massive change. Today, I want you to do one thing that you find uncomfortable. Pick up that phone, and ask out that person you find attractive. Whatever it is, do it TODAY!

The best way to keep your comfort zone in a continual state of growth is to strive towards doing one thing each and every day that you find uncomfortable. Just keep doing things that make you a little nervous and, before long, you will find that you do it with ease as it has now become part of your comfort zone, which means it's time to start doing other things that are uncomfortable.

There are many things that can get in our way, but they are not boulders that block our road. They are just stepping-stones in our journey, and you now have the skills and the insight to ensure that you use them to help, not hinder, you in your journey.

Chapter Eight

NOW FLOOR IT

Life is yours

> " It's not knowing what to do,
> it's doing what you know
> — Anthony Robbins "

If you have read this book from start to finish, it's now almost time to put me down. You see, you are at the stage where you must take the next step. You must DO.

Your first steps on your journey will be full of excitement and enthusiasm. The trick is keeping that right through to the one hundred and fifteenth step.

Too often, people attend seminars, get all enthused, but do nothing with that knowledge or enthusiasm. And two years later, their lives haven't changed, because they didn't take ACTION.

Don't let that be you with the knowledge you have learnt from this book. If you are feeling excitement and a sense of control now due to this book, know that I am thrilled, as that was the purpose of this book – to motivate, educate and excite you. Don't let the feeling fade. Take action on the knowledge, put it into practice and reinforce it into habit and your overall personality.

Right now, I want you to think about one aspect, just one aspect, that you have learnt from this book that you would like to implement in your life. It may be seeing the positives in everything, or learning a new skill you've always wanted to learn, or overriding a self-limiting belief with a new, positive belief. Remember, on average, it takes 21 days to create a habit, so pick just one area to focus on at first, and start today. In 21 days, you will have changed not just one, but numerous aspects of your life, because as you now know, it's all interrelated – a single change affects many areas.

On a final note, I would like you to remember something that I wish others had told me.

You will fall into your old ways occasionally. Don't beat yourself up about it. There are still many times when I come across a situation and FEAR takes over. I remind myself of the true meaning of fear. I know it is just False Expectations Appearing Real and that I'm just Finding Excuses And Reasons. Yet, on occasion, I do not find the strength to push myself through those limiting beliefs and fears. We are all on a journey, and it doesn't matter how far down your journey you get. There will be the occasional bumps in the road. The key is persistence. Never stop growing. Always be improving and striving to be the best in all aspects of your life.

So many people are living in unchartered waters; they have no real map and don't know what lies ahead.

You, however, now do!

BE who you want to be, DO what you need to do, in order to HAVE the life you want to have.

The past does not equal your future. No one can go back and make a brand new start, but you can decide to act now to make a brand new ending.

You have the knowledge. You know what the next steps are.

So what are you waiting for? Go out there and <u>drive your life</u>!

There are $183 of Bonus Gifts Waiting for You...

Recommended Further Reading

Books

- *Think and Grow Rich* – Napoleon Hill

- *The Magic of Thinking Big* – David J. Schwartz

- *Law of Attraction* – Michael J. Losier

- *The 7 Habits of Highly Effective People* – Stephen R. Covey

- *The Dip* – Seth Godin

- *Billionaire in Training* – Bradley J. Sugars

- *The 4-Hour Work Week* – Tim Ferris

- *Awaken the Giant Within* – Anthony Robbins

Websites

- http://www.entrepreneursuccessclub.com

- http://www.kaizenseries.com

- http://www.succcess.org (please note the three C's)

There are $183 of Bonus Gifts Waiting for You...

Final Thoughts

Congratulations, you have now learnt the key concepts and steps to turning your current life into the life of your dreams.

Always remember, the destination is an exciting place but the journey along the way is just as exciting and should be enjoyed every step of the way.

Life is fun, and should always be fun. Get serious at times when necessary, certainly, but do it with a sense of fun remaining as well.

I encourage you to join the Kaizen club on www. kaizenseries.com to claim your free bonuses and share your goals and experiences with the community.

Until next time, live life 110%.

Carl Taylor

How to Claim Your Free Gift

FREE GIFT #1 ($35.00 value)
101 Powerful Affirmations to a More Positive You
This Quick Read gives you a valuable list of 101 Positive Affirmations that will change your life dramatically, take them straight from this book or use them as examples to structure you own.

FREE GIFT #2 ($37.00 Value)
Living Your Ultimate Life - Dream Builder
This workbook will take you through getting clear on your dreams, what do you truly want to have in life. By getting clear on this then you can set to work at doing what you need to do and being who you need to be.

FREE GIFT #3 ($15.00 Value)
Commiting to Action
A special report on how to best commit to your actions, who to tell, when and why.

FREE GIFT #4 ($27.00 Value)
Decision Score Card
Are you an effective decision maker? Are there areas of decision making you need to improve in? Find out with this Decision Score Card software.

FREE GIFT #5 ($69.00 Value)
Goal Setting Templates
Everything you need to effectively set your goals using the Goal Setting Heirarchy as discussed in Red Means Go!, Daily Todo Sheets, Breaking them down piece by piece.

Download at:
www.KaizenSeries.com/RMG

There are $183 of Bonus Gifts Waiting for You...

About the Author

Carl Taylor was once a shy and introverted boy who then discovered Kaizen. After years of learning from great mentors, reading countless books and attending numerous seminars on wealth, business, finance, goal setting and personal development, his life has transformed.

Carl started his first business at the age of 15. Since then, he has owned numerous different businesses in many industries, founded the "Entrepreneur Success Club" and has coached business owners and individuals in business and life skills. Throughout his journey, he has learnt many skills and faced limiting beliefs – both his own and the ones imposed by others.

Carl's purpose in life is to be the best he can be, and to help others be the best that they can be.

It is because of this purpose that the Kaizen Series exists, and through his passion, people's lives all around the world are changing for the better.

You can learn more about Carl at www.carltaylor.com.au

www.ingramcontent.com/pod-product-compliance
Lightning Source LLC
Chambersburg PA
CBHW060543100426
42742CB00013B/2437